BIT HORSE

Brenton Healy

Chapter 1

Kenneth Farewood rents an apartment unit in a pink building in a rough part of Los Angeles, California. He's sitting behind a computer at his desk, asleep, when someone knocks on his door and wakes him up.

"Trojan! Trojan!...Open up!" the voice calls.

Kenneth goes by the nickname Trojan. It's what people call him in the Underground. As soon as he opens the door, he sees Viper, his pal from the Underground, standing there.

"Yo, Viper!" Trojan says. "I thought you were the apartment manager about to bug me for being late on the rent."

"...Dude, that sounds like a personal problem," Viper replies. "I just need to pick up the hard drive...And did you have a minute to talk?"

Kenneth, who had been heading inside to bring the hard drive to him, stops for a minute. "Yeah, sure. What's up?"

"There's a new list that came in on the register. I'm going to need you to use your skills to get a bite on the hook." Viper is referring to hacking the people "Upstairs"—people on the surface of the cyber world, who those in the Underground victimize for their wealth and identities.

Trojan realizes this is a great opportunity to make some money and agrees to go back with Viper to the Underground. He grabs the hard drive and hastily leaves the apartment with his friend.

Before long they enter what looks like it used to be a hole-in-the-wall nightclub, but has since been abandoned and given over to rats. All of the walls have some kind of tagging on them. This is a place that attracts misfits and drug addicts, but also mostly computer hackers.

As the pair walk down a hallway, they're approached by a security guard. This is a special part of the building. He recognizes Viper and Trojan, but checks if anyone snuck in behind them before giving them access to go further down the hallway. They move past him into a small room where there are people with colored hair, wearing windbreakers and sitting around tables with desktops and laptops in front of them.

The two sit at Viper's station and Viper shows Trojan the list of prospects he'd obtained. These unsuspecting people are from Upstairs, and they'll use a program called Bit Horse to hack their identities and sensitive information, then sell it to bidders on the black market. Viper downloads the list onto the hard drive and then, done with their business, they leave the room.

Walking past the guard, they go back the way they came in. Trojan tells Viper, "This is going to make us a lot more money than I thought, I'm sure of it."

Viper agrees. "Just as soon as I contact my guy and find bidders, we'll be set in motion."

"Sure thing," says Trojan. "I'll get back to you after the weekend. I'm gonna need to spend some time on this."

Once they've left the headquarters of the Underground, they split up and head their own ways.

Chapter 2

Back at his apartment, Kenneth plugs in the hard drive that he'd been going to lend Viper before he got involved with this. He knew that it was for this purpose, so Viper didn't need it anymore. He looks at the names on the list and to his surprise, sees a familiar name: Billy Waltzer. He opens up his file and sure enough, it's somebody he had classes with in junior college. Suddenly he doesn't feel like going through with this—he knew Billy, and the guy was a good one.

Kenneth flashes back to a time when he and Billy shared a conversation about their plans for the future. Billy had said he wanted to be a counselor and help broken people who needed the support. Kenneth remembers talking about his own plans to teach people how to use computers. Thinking about it now, he feels discouraged about his involvement in the Underground and the hacking world. He decides to sleep on it before he chooses whether to go through with it or not. He calls it a night and goes to bed.

The next morning, Kenneth wakes up to a text message making his cell phone buzz. He picks it up. The message was sent by an anonymous person and reads, "Is the hook in?" Kenneth knows it's from Viper, but he hasn't had any time to work on the hack since he found Billy's name on the list. He decides it's probably okay to go ahead with it and Kenneth decides to reply—"They'll bite soon."

He gets up, goes across the hallway and sits at his desk in his office. He logs in to his computer and gets to work. Opening up the hacking program, he finds the list and scans for data that would be potentially valuable to a bidder on the black market.

After a while, he collects the data from the program and puts it on a secure disc drive dedicated to storing a terabyte of sensitive and classified information. Next he emails Viper with the message, "It's time—meet up at Underground ASAP—Trojan."

Kenneth gets up, puts the disc drive into a pocket in his bag and puts on his black hooded sweatshirt. Then he slings the bag over his shoulder and walks out the door.

Chapter 3

Viper is already at the Underground by the time Kenneth arrives. Kenneth comes running up to him in front of the headquarters, carrying his bag.

"Hey!" Viper says. "I got the message. Let's do this! It's all set up." Together, they walk into the building.

They go to Viper's station and log into Bit Horse. Trojan hesitates and looks at Viper, thinking about Billy Waltzer, but goes ahead and inserts the disc drive into the USB port. All the files pop up and they go through the collected data on each individual. Viper, who has been waiting eagerly for this, says, "These people don't know what'll hit them!"

Kenneth says, "You know, I feel bad about how we're benefiting from all these people at their expense. They really have no clue what we're up to."

Viper rolls his eyes at him. "You know how corrupt this Underground can be. People like us aren't meant to do anything else but hack. Besides, those people up there are just as crooked as us, but in other ways. We're just honest about it."

Kenneth disagrees. "As crooked as us! You don't know what you're talking about!"

"Look...if you think for a second they're all angels Upstairs, then you ought to just quit this racket and be one yourself," Viper tells him.

"I know I'm not one," Kenneth says, "but maybe I should just leave the Underground, because this racket is corrupt. It's like a rat circus, and we're just a bunch of rats in it, leeching off of people that are more decent and civilized than us."

Viper looks down at the floor and Kenneth exits the room, leaving his bag on the table.

Chapter 4

Kenneth goes into an internet lounge in the city and orders a cup of coffee at the counter, then sits down at one of the desks with his laptop. He searches for Billy Waltzer on the internet and finds him. After clicking around a while, Kenneth's search brings him to the website of his old junior college, Still Creek Community College, where Billy was also a student. Now, Billy is a counselor of the student body there.

Kenneth looks up what room to find Billy in at Still Creek and writes it down. Then he heads out to look for him. When he gets to the school, he goes to room 305 in Building F and asks the receptionist if Counselor Billy Waltzer is in today.

"Oh, he's out to lunch," she says. "He'll be back in 45 minutes." So Kenneth waits on the steps and after about an hour, he sees Billy walk by.

"Counselor Waltzer?" Kenneth says, getting up to stop him. "I'm Kenneth Farewood. I took 4th period Computer Science with you back when I went to school here. Do you remember me?"

Billy looks at him. "Oh yes! That was a long time ago. I remember now, you used to talk to me when I was sitting by myself in the corner, tryin' to pass the class. I've moved on now, I have a wife and two children. I have my own office here where I help students find the right path for their education."

"That's so great," Kenneth replies. "You told me that. I believed in you."

"What's that you say?"

"You told me that you wanted to be a counselor to people that didn't have guidance in life, and that's what you've been doing, I see."

Billy looks at him. "And you? What have you chosen as your path in life?"

Kenneth looks away. "Computers...I'm pretty good with computers."

Billy smiles. "That's a good thing." But Kenneth can't explain that he's a computer hacker and that Billy's name is on the register in the Underground.

Instead he says, "Maybe we could get some coffee sometime and catch up." And Billy agrees.

Chapter 5

Now that Kenneth has left the Underground and his cyber identity as Trojan behind, he starts looking for new work. He sees an ad on a poster for a company called Antica Corp. They're a startup and need to build a team of software programmers. He thinks a job working with computers at the business level might be something he wants, so he calls the number on the poster and talks to a recruiter about the position. He tells them that he is good with computers and they go ahead and schedule him an Interview for the next day.

He shows up to the interview and does the Q and A with the recruiter from Antica Corp. Seeing that he has knowledge about computer software, they sign him up immediately. The company looks promising to Kenneth and he's excited for the opportunity to go legitimate with his talents.

Kenneth gets his new office and after a while, has gotten acquainted with this new startup company. But one day, he looks through his window into the common area and spots his ex-hacker buddy Viper. Viper, going by the name Tom, is walking next to Mr. Richardson, who is the recruiter that signed Kenneth on with Antica Corp. It looks like bad news to Kenneth, and he closes the blinds to his office.

Tom gets hired, but he'll be working on a different floor, so Kenneth thinks he can dodge him. He decides he'll avoid ever having to go to that floor, lest his past be found out and he lose his job.

But later that afternoon, Kenneth runs into Tom on the street outside the building where they now both work. Tom says, "Hey what are you doin' here?"

"I work here now," Kenneth reluctantly tells him. "What are you doing here?"

Tom replies, "Antica Corp. approached me. They know I'm a hacker, and they offered to let me work in their secret department, where they use me and other hackers from the Underground to eliminate their competition in the software industry. It's all a part of their expansion plan to go public."

Kenneth realizes that this was a trap for him, and he doesn't like it at all. He thinks that maybe Viper was right about the Upstairs being just as corrupt as the

Underground, just in a different way. This is a problem—Kenneth sees no hope in staying with the company, so he quits his job. He needs to talk to someone. He immediately thinks of Counselor Waltzer, and how he never took him up on the offer to get some coffee and catch up on their lives since junior college.

So he decides to email him.

Chapter 6

A week after quitting his job with Antica Corp., Kenneth meets with Billy Waltzer at a coffee bar downtown and explains everything. He tells Billy about the Underground hacking community he was a part of, how he came across Billy's information, and how it's been stored on the black market.

Billy expresses uneasiness when he hears this disturbing news. He thinks maybe he should call the police and turn Kenneth in, but he also understands that Kenneth is coming clean with him. He decides that Kenneth is the one who has the real problems, and chooses to overlook the dark things Kenneth has brought up. He forgives Kenneth and tells him, "If your heart is seeking a way to correct these things you've done, then my suggestion is to live on a path that's truly for you and work at being the best version of yourself... always. If your old identity is the problem, then find a new way to overcome it. The real you knows where you ought to be. So listen to what your heart tells you and make the change.

"It's been nice catching up with you, Kenneth. So long."

Then Billy walks away while Kenneth sits there a while longer, asking himself questions about what matters to him most. He thinks about talking to Billy in junior college, and a lightbulb clicks on in his mind. Before he got into hacking, all he wanted to do was teach people about computers. With that in his mind, he gets up and goes home.

Chapter 7

Weeks after his meeting with Counselor Waltzer, Kenneth goes back to Still Creek Community College and applies for a teaching position in their computer science program. He's been wanting to go legitimate with his computer skills, and now he sees that this is the way to make his dreams come true.

He hears back from the college later that week—they have approved him as a teacher. Ecstatic, he starts thanking God for what has been accomplished. He's now officially a contributor to society, and has defeated the ghosts of his past that kept him from a realer form of success and happiness.

To conclude, if there is one thing to learn from this book, it is to be honest with yourself and others. Only then will you prevail, in any path you choose.

The End